Archaeopteryx
Ancient Wings

Dinosaur Books for Young Readers

By Enrique Fiesta
Mendon Cottage Books

JD-Biz Publishing

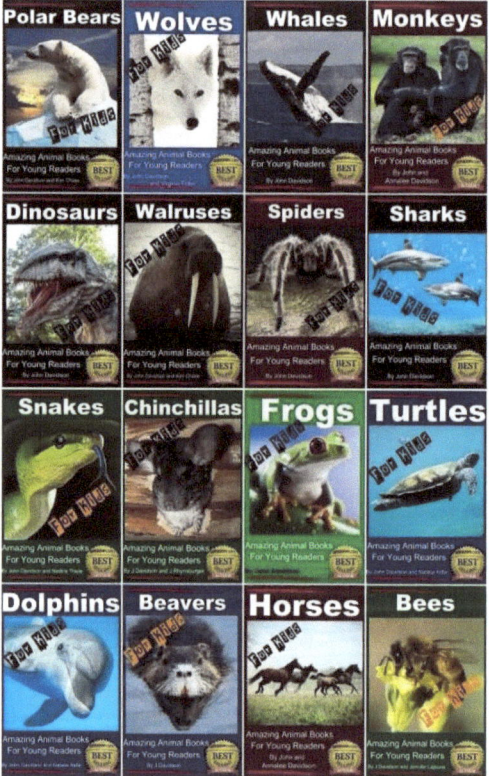

Download Free Books!
http://MendonCottageBooks.com

Table of Contents

Introduction

Greetings young reader! Today we are going to take a step back in time and enter the age of the dinosaurs. The dinosaurs are an extinct species of animal that began to live on the Earth over 200 million years ago. "Extinct" means that they no longer exist. The dinosaurs are some of the most intriguing and awe-inspiring animals that have existed on our planet. The dinosaurs' colossal size, strange characteristics, and mysterious disappearance make them *inherently* worthy of study and interest. Even more than these reasons, the study of dinosaurs itself is an incredible adventure which requires thought and imagination. The study of dinosaurs helps you to appreciate just how mysterious and amazing life and nature really is. Our planet supports not only us and the animals that live today, but it even supported creatures as gigantic and strange as the dinosaurs- just think how cool that is! I hope that you bring a spirit of openness and wonder to your study of the dinosaurs, and that you come to appreciate the mystery and value of the dinosaurs.

Today we are going to take a look at an incredibly fascinating dinosaur called the Archaeopteryx. The Archaeopteryx is receiving a lot of attention today by scientists and paleontologists because of its dual nature: it was not only a dinosaur, but it was also one of the very first birds! This dinosaur's status makes it a crucial to the evolutionary theory. Evolution is the theoretical process through which living things are thought to have come into existence. We will discuss this theory in the pages to come. We are not only going to talk about the Archaeopteryx's relationship to evolutionary theory, but also about what the Archaeopteryx looked like, how it behaved, where and when it lived, and even about the plants and animals it shared its habitat with. We know what we know about the dinosaurs from a variety of sources including fossils, biology, and other scientific disciplines. Fossils are the ancient remains of the dinosaurs, the most familiar being their bones. Biological science is the study of life in general, but many scientists compare the dinosaurs to modern day animals to support their theories.

Chapter 1: Appearance

The Archaeopteryx is an interesting dinosaur because it shares characteristics with the ancient dinosaurs *and* characteristics of modern day birds. Because of the Archaeopteryx's birdlike and reptile like characteristics many scientists believe that it represents a stage between the dinosaurs and modern day birds. In order to understand why the Archaeopteryx is considering an "in-between stage" it is crucial to understand what evolution is.

Evolution is the process by which living things are believed to have developed from earlier living things during the history of the earth. This means that the animals that live today are actually the descendants of life forms that existed millions of years ago. Scientists believe that today's birds are actually the descendants of the dinosaurs. Through gradual change, some of the ancient dinosaurs became birds. Scientists believe that the Archaeopteryx represents an in-between stage of the ancient dinosaurs' gradual change into the birds we know and love today!

The Archaeopteryx was small and light just like many modern day birds. It could reach a length of about 20 inches and a weight of about one pound. The Archaeopteryx shared many other characteristics with modern day birds like a "wish-bone." The wish-bone is a forked bone in front of the breastbone in birds- it is the bone that people break during Thanksgiving. The purpose of the bone is to hold strong muscles together; for birds in particular, the strong muscles are the wing muscles. Several other dinosaurs had wishbones including the Tyrannosaurus Rex, for whom the wishbone probably held together powerful arm muscles. The wishbone of the Archaeopteryx, like the birds, held together the wing muscles. The Archaeopteryx was also covered in feathers. The presence of a wishbone and feathers (wing and tail feathers) suggest that the Archaeopteryx was fully capable of flight, or at least capable of gliding. Gliding is the ability to soar great distances using the wind, as opposed to flight which is the ability to remain airborne using wings and muscle power.

The Archaeopteryx was different from modern day birds in several respects as well. Modern day birds have horny, toothless beaks; the Archaeopteryx had slim jaws lined with curved, sharp teeth. It also had a long, bony tail whereas modern day birds do not. The feathers on the tail formed something like a fan, in that the feathers grew from the sides and end of the tail. The Archaeopteryx also had three fingers tipped with sharp claws, similar to dinosaurs and dissimilar to modern day birds.

The color of the Archaeopteryx is unknown but there are many hypothetical possibilities. Birds today range in color from completely black (blackbird) to every color of the rainbow (think parrot). The Archaeopteryx could have been the same color of its environment in order to be camouflaged in its environment, or it could have been decoratively colored like many birds today. Unfortunately, we will probably never know *exactly* what color Archaeopteryx was.

Chapter 2: Behavior

The Archaeopteryx was a predator just like most birds are today. A predator is an animal that hunts other animals for food. A predator's hunted food source is called its prey. It was probably omnivorous which means that it ate just about anything. It would have eaten prey smaller than itself such as insects and small reptile. It is also possible that it ate nuts, seeds, and fruits. Scientific reports indicate that the Archaeopteryx was diurnal. Diurnal means "active during the day." It most likely awoke in the morning, hunted during the day, and slept at night.

The Archaeopteryx was an egg-laying animal like most dinosaurs, birds, and reptiles. It is possible that the Archaeopteryx built nests like modern birds but there is no fossilized evidence to support this idea.

The Archaeopteryx most likely used to ability to fly/glide to catch its prey unawares. If it was able to fly, it is probable that it would swoop down on prey and quickly catch it between its jaws. The claws of the Archaeopteryx are sharp, which means it could climb trees with ease (like a squirrel). If prey was larger than a lizard or insect, it would have used its sharp claws to grasp the prey.

If the Archaeopteryx had colorful feathers it was most likely limited to the males. This is because many modern-day bird species which have colorful feathers limit this characteristic to the males. The colorful males use their vibrant feathers to attract potential mates. If the Archaeopteryx was colorful it, too, would have used its colors to attract female mates; however, it is still unknown what color the Archaeopteryx was. If the Archaeopteryx was the same color as its environment it was probably a combination of black, brown, or tan like most birds are today. Black, brown, and tan colorations allow most predators to surprise prey, because the predator blends in with its surroundings.

It is unknown whether the Archaeopteryx lived primarily in vegetation (such as trees and shrubs) or on the ground. Scientists argue this point, but it seems that the Archaeopteryx could have lived in either without too much difficulty (based on the fossils).

Chapter 3: Environment

All Archaeopteryx fossils were found in Bavaria, Germany in Solnhofen. The Archaeopteryx lived in the Late Jurassic Period about 156-150 million years ago. The Jurassic Period is the middle period of the Mesozoic Era. The Mesozoic Era lasted between 245-213 million years ago and is divided into three periods: the Triassic, Jurassic, and Cretaceous Periods. During this time the seven continents were closer together, the climate was hotter, and there were no polar ice caps. The ancestors of animals today lived in this period (the ancestor of the bird possibly being the Archaeopteryx). At the end of the Cretaceous Period all dinosaurs (save for birds) ceased to exist probably due to a combination of factors such as meteoric impacts, climate change, and disease.

The Archaeopteryx specifically lived in salty, stagnant lagoons within tropical oceans. The lagoons were semi-arid and sub-tropical. This means that the area received little precipitation (rainfall) but was still humid. A lagoon in a shallow body of water separated from oceans by islands or coral reefs. They are salt-water environments. The Archaeopteryx lived on islands within the lagoon, but could most hop from island to island by flying. The watery environment would make one think that the Archaeopteryx ate fish, but scientists believe the salty lagoon would have been too salty for fish to thrive in. The Archaeopteryx, although being able to fly, was probably not a strong enough to swoop down and catch fish prey from out of the ocean.

These two evidentiary claims make scientists conclude that the Archaeopteryx did not eat fish, like other flying dinosaurs (pterosaurs).

The Archaeopteryx lived with a host of other Late Jurassic dinosaurs which it either hunted, was hunted by, or lived peaceably with. Some other dinosaurs that lived in what is now Europe during the Late Jurassic include the Camarasaurus, the Compsognathus, and the pterosaurs.

The Camarasaurus is a sauropod. A sauropod was a long necked, long tailed herbivorous dinosaur with strong thick legs, a large torso, and a small head. Herbivorous means that it ate vegetation. The Camarasaurus reached a length of about fifty feet and weight of about fifty tons making it longer and heavier than the average school bus. It was one of the largest dinosaurs of the Late Jurassic. It is possible that Archaeopteryx would have flown in the skies above these majestic dinosaurs.

The Compsognathus was a small, speedy predatory built a lot like the Archaeopteryx. The two would have competed for prey if they lived in the same areas. The Compsognathus, like Archaeopteryx, possessed slim jaws, sharp teeth, and sharp claws. It lacked the wings of the Archaeopteryx but it may also have been covered in feathers. It is possible that the two might have hunted each other.

The other flying dinosaur of the Late Jurassic was the pterosaur. The pterosaurs lacked feathers and were instead covered in scales. Instead of feathered wings they possessed leathery wings with which they used to fly. They ranged in size as some were the size of pigeons while others were the size of eagles and other raptors (the name for birds of prey). The largest pterosaur had a wingspan of 36 feet making it larger than small air planes. It is possible that the Archaeopteryx fed on small pterosaurs, but it is also likely that larger pterosaurs would have hunted Archaeopteryx. The two shared the skies together in the Late Jurassic Period.

Conclusion

We have stepped back in time to look at this dinosaur, where and when he lived, and the dinosaurs he lived with- and what a journey it was! By using our imaginations and knowledge we can engage, wonder about, and appreciate the wonderful mystery and value of the dinosaurs. By learning about and appreciating what the dinosaurs were we come to appreciate our own present age and all the wonderful creatures that live today. We discover how varied and mysterious life really is- we look at animals today with a newfound appreciation and awe. Make sure you keep thinking, learning, and imagining, and *really* make sure that you never lose your sense of wonder.

Author Bio

Enrique Fiesta

I was born in Southwest Florida and I hold a degree in Latin and Greek language and literature. In addition to my principal studies, I have also studied philosophy, history, the natural sciences, and literature. In my spare time I devote the vast majority of my time to reading, writing, praying, and walking. I am currently pursuing legal studies in order to become an attorney. After I earn my law degree I intend to pursue a doctorate in philosophy, literature, and politics.

Our books are available at

1. Amazon.com

2. Barnes and Noble

3. Itunes

4. Kobo

5. Smashwords

6. Google Play Books

Download Free Books!
http://MendonCottageBooks.com

Publisher

JD-Biz Corp

P O Box 374

Mendon, Utah 84325

http://www.jd-biz.com/

www.ingramcontent.com/pod-product-compliance
Lightning Source LLC
Chambersburg PA
CBHW050930290526
45792CB00002B/960